E V E

Books by Annie Finch

POETRY
Eve
Catching the Mermother
The Encyclopedia of Scotland

CRITICISM
The Ghost of Meter: Culture and Prosody
in American Free Verse

ANTHOLOGIES
A Formal Feeling Comes: Poems in Form
by Contemporary Women

E V E

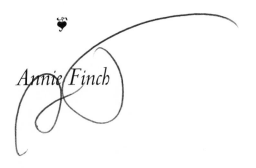

Annie Finch

Story Line Press
1 9 9 7

Published by Story Line Press, Inc.,
Three Oaks Farm/PO Box 1240, Ashland, OR 97520-0055

This publication was made possible thanks in part to the gen-
erous support of the Nicholas Roerich Museum, the Andrew
W. Mellon Foundation, and our individual contributors.

Book design by Chiquita Babb

Library of Congress Cataloging-in-Publication Data

Finch, Annie, 1956–
         Eve / Annie Finch
              p. cm.
         ISBN 1-885266-36-7.—ISBN 1-885266-46-4 (pbk.)
         1. Goddesses—Poetry. 2. Family—Poetry. 3. Women—Poetry.
      I. Title.
      PS33556.1448E8 1997
      811'.54—dc21   97-925
                                                                          CIP

for C. A. K.
with gratitude

ACKNOWLEDGMENTS

Many people have helped me during the time I was bringing these poems to their present form. For advice, inspiration, or encouragement in my work as a poet, I am gratefully indebted to colleagues and companions, students and mentors, editors and critics too numerous to name. For various kinds of help with this book, I would like to mention my thanks to David Baker, Frances Brown, Penelope Laurans, Robert McDowell, Denise Mosley, Ntozake Shange, Timothy Steele, and Marie Truscott, and my colleagues at Miami University. Special thanks to the College of Arts and Sciences of Miami University for their support. As for my thanks to Dana Gioia, Carolyn Kizer, Robin Leanse, and Molly Peacock, it knows "no lapse, nor Diminution—." Special thanks to Alix Baer Bacon, Roy Finch Jr., Roy and Margaret Finch, Julian Finch-Brand, and Susan Landau for patience and support during hard times. Glen Brand has helped bring this book to life many times over; my appreciation and gratitude are as boundless as his insight and generosity.

Poems in this book have appeared previously in the following publications, very often in substantially different versions:

Agni Review: "Being a Constellation," "Running in Church"; *Caprice:* "Gulf War and Child" (as "Riddle: War and Child"); *Cincinnati Poetry Review:* "The Circled Sand"; *Deviance:* "Diving Past Violets" (as "Diving in African Violets"); *The Dark Horse* (Scotland): "Running in Church"; *Evil Dog:* "Aphrodite"; *The Formalist:* "Coy Mistress" (as "A Reply From His Coy Mistress)," "Sapphics for Patience" (as "Sapphics"), "Still Life"; *Kansas Quarterly:* "Settler" (as "The Native American Birds"); *Kenyon Review:* "Samhain," "Three Generations of Secrets"; *The MacGuffin:* "Westminster" (as "Among Monuments"); *Many Mountains Moving:* "Hostage Wildflowers," "Daughter" (as "Whirling"); *Nebo:* "In Cities, Be Alert," "Lucid Waking"; *Osiris:* "Tribute" (as "Dickinson"); *Outposts Poetry Quarterly* (England): "The Garden" (as "An Anglo-Saxon Garden"); *Paris Review:* "Great Reading Room Murals"; *Partisan Review:* "Courtship"; *Plains*

Poetry Journal: "Another Reluctance"; *Poetry Flash:* "My Raptor"; *Poets On . . . Forgetting:* "Still Life"; *Puerto del Sol:* "The Wish for Eyes"; *Sequoia:* "Rain Birth"; *South Carolina Review:* "Ancestor," "Pearl" (as "Pearls"); *South Coast Poetry Journal:* "Catching the Mermother"; *South Dakota Review:* "No Snake"; *Southwest Review:* "Inside the Violet"; *Sparrow:* "Still Life" (as "The Pitcher"), "My Raptor"; *Tennessee Quarterly:* "Strangers" (as "Mardi Gras"), "Thanksgiving"; *Thirteen:* "The Door" (as "Episcopalian Dream"); *A Formal Feeling Comes: Poems in Form by Contemporary Women:* "Tribute" (as "Dickinson"), "Ancestor" (as "For Grizzel McNaught"), "Sapphics for Patience," "Coy Mistress" (as "A Reply From His Coy Mistress"); *Introduction to Literature* and *Introduction to Poetry* (8th editions): "Tribute" (as "Dickinson"); *The Muse Strikes Back: Women Reply to Poems by Men:* "Coy Mistress"; *Prayers to Protest: Poems that Center and Bless Us:* "The Door," "Thanksgiving"; *Telling the Barn Swallow: Essays in Honor of Maxine Kumin:* "Zaraf's Star"; *The Unitarian Universalist Poets: A Contemporary American Survey:* "Running in Church." "Being a Constellation," "Mermother," "Coy Mistress," "Diving Past African Violets," "Lucid Waking," "Tribute," "My Raptor," "No Snake," "Pearls," "Samhain," and "Sapphics for Patience" appeared as *Catching the Mermother* (Aralia Press, 1997).

The nine italicized poems, written as a sequence entitled "The Furious Sun in Her Mane," have been set to music by Laura Beck and choreographed for nine dancers by Georgia Bonatis. The piece was performed several times in Iowa and New York during 1994.

CONTENTS

Rhiannon   1

Running in Church   2

No Snake   3

Zaraf's Star   4

Spider Woman   7

Lucid Waking   8

My Raptor   9

Great Reading Room Murals   10

The Door   11

Inanna   13

The Last Mermother   14

Daughter   16

Strangers   17

Westminster   18

Coatlique   21

Still Life   22

The Circled Sand   23

In Cities, Be Alert   24

Insect   25

Three Generations of Secrets   26

Brigid   27

Sapphics for Patience   28

Inside the Violet   29

Pearl   30

Rain Birth   31

Nut   33

Frozen In *34*

The Garden *35*

Another Reluctance *36*

Tribute *37*

Aphrodite *39*

Courtship *40*

Coy Mistress *41*

Being a Constellation *42*

Walk With Me *43*

Changing Woman *45*

Ancestor *46*

Gulf War and Child: A Curse *47*

Thanksgiving *48*

The Wish for Eyes *50*

Eve *51*

Encounter *52*

Samhain *53*

Diving Past Violets *55*

Notes on the Poems *57*

EVE

RHIANNON

A child is ranging, like a young horse;
a child is growing, like a gray mare.
She carries the coastal wind in her teeth
and the furious sun in her mane.

RUNNING IN CHURCH

for Marie

Then, you were a hot-thinking, thin-lidded tinderbox.
Losing your balance meant nothing at all. You would
pour through the aisles in the highest cathedrals,
careening deftly as patriarchs brooded.

You made the long corridors ring, tintinnabular
echoes exploring the pounded cold floor,
forcing the walls to the truth of your progress:
there was a person in this church's core.

Past thick stained-glass colors wafted and swirling
in pooled interludes that swung down from the rafters,
cinnabar wounds threw light on your face, where the
pliant young bones were dissolving in laughter.

NO SNAKE

Inside my Eden I can find no snake.
There's not one I could look to and believe,
obey and then be ruined by and leave
because of, bearing children and an ache.

I circle down on Eden from above,
searching the fields in solitude and love
like a high hawk. She would never forsake

this place that's made again of memory;
she'd wait in that tree below me, spring
out towards my growing shadow, let it bring
a sudden hope that she could coil free;

but she's not here. Only mountains that curve,
and dip around the valley when I swerve,
settle with dark heights, as I near the tree.

ZARAF'S STAR

Walking changes as dusk starts to gather.
We're not able or sure anymore.
We don't know the path—and if we did know it,

we wouldn't go on. We're afraid of the dark
lowering its heavy, long familiarity
down on the grass. We're afraid of the night,

moonless, desert, California,
making us stumble. We shouldn't be lost,
out here like demons just at the border

that touches us solid, as if we were gone.
She's leading me on a path as narrow
as sisters can share. We pound back down the mesa.

Each of our feet finds its own way, delving
into the gulley whose trees never answer
until, with steps slapping soft as bandits,

I slow on the path, imagining horses.

Stretching necks right out of the stones,
out of the dusk where dark has achieved our
bodies, drawn by the strides that my sister

takes like a rider, Zaraf's Star,
Fashad, Kashmir, Arabian horses
raise her up with motionless shadow

so she can ride (like a rider, she walks),
cantering, encompassing the pace of the mountain.
Out in a landscape to curl or be curled in,

hunched like riders or curling like rides,
under the fairy-tale oaks of the mesa
that hide sleeping children or horses inside,

we talk about horses like hers who run carefully,
with thinner ankles, and mustangs who, fast,
wild grown, wild on the path to blackness,

hunger like stars reaching down for dark leaves.

SPIDER WOMAN

Your thoughts in a web have covered the sky.
A thread from the northwest is carrying beads from the rain,
a thread from the southwest is carrying beads from the rain,
a thread from the southeast carries bright beads,
a thread from the northeast is bringing the beads
of the rain that has filled up the sky.
Spider, you have woven a chain
stretching with rain over the sky.

LUCID WAKING

Once I wanted the whole dawn not to let me
sleep. One morning, then, I awoke and watched as
waking woke me, came slipping up through half-light
crying softly, a cat leaving her corner,
stretching, tall in the new gray air of morning,
raising paws much too high. She came slow-stepping
down the hallway to crouch, to call, to answer
through the door, making still and slow the dawning
once so bird-ridden—and the sun, the curtains—

MY RAPTOR

My mind hovered over my baby, like
a raptor, and froze everything it saw.
I looked through my own pregnant belly's raw
perimeters and found his heart to strike
attentive until, helpless with the pound
of still more blood, he seemed to settle down.
It was my loss to feel like god alone
for a new one always listening, to reach
inside for his ears to share the flying speech
I heard so constantly. Within my grown
silence, my sounding, my loud body where
the baby turned, my mind learned not to care
whether thoughts I felt he noticed with no fear
were mine alone—or whether he could hear.

GREAT READING ROOM MURALS

Knowledge is lost and generous. Here she sits,
bracing her legs like pillars so they'll hold
the book she opens, peeking at Peace's old
wrinkled face, letting the jesters and the wits
encircle her, and watching the Great Red Spirit's
wooden-limbed presence loom on the books and gold,
the overwhelming fruits just now unrolled
from Progress's advancing chariots
as dazzled Natives hide their eyes. This room
spins on its murals, dragging her vision past
heads bowed toward books whose turning pages hide
truth with each tiny rustle. Teachers whom
our words depend on taunt her with their vast
ennobled pain; we read on by their side.

THE DOOR

It seemed as if a door came calling,
in a voice as old as carols,
telling lies as old as candles,
in words that were all about
some afternoons, lost on a child,
that could have been simple but
were lost, when I was just a child.

There was a day and then a dream
that I went through, and a cathedral
whose tall choir prayed
a singing message through the nave
until I heard a forest there
(though far outside, the trees were bare)

INANNA

A young goddess, full of love, fresh with the touch of a husband,
carrying power and rich with anger, strength, urgency, understanding,
follows the direction her ear has led her, down to the place where the
underworld glistens.

A goddess goes down, and I can see her. She needs to go, decides to go.
A goddess goes down, and I can hear her.

At each door she removes a jewel, a belt, a ceremonial robe.
At each door, she is less and more. She bows down through the seventh
door.

The young goddess is dead, and waiting. The young goddess is dead.
A goddess goes down, and I can see her. She needs to go, decides to go.
A goddess goes down, and I can hear her.

THE LAST MERMOTHER

I used to fish in San Francisco Bay,
without a net, for love as well as food.
Out by the water, on a long, cool day,
I had a place to go, and some time to brood.
The only woman usually, I glued
my hands to the rod. They left me alone; I enjoyed
those days, until the day I was destroyed.

It started with a tentative tug, slow, confined
without a glance or the pressure of a hand.
Then it teased me like a simple, other mind
across my own, vibrating in command.
Then I almost fell, as she charged high, and fanned
open her tailfins, arching through the spray
of her own raging white wake. Don't look away;

listen. I breathed, and she tore away the line
and raised her face—those empty eyes—beside
the dock. She howled, stretching her hand to mine,
floating her tail in the rocking of the tide
as she clung to the slippery post below. I tried
to look at her. I saw that it was true.
Well, what would you have done? I helped her through

the railing. Draped with clammy seaweed strands,
she wiggled her huge shoulders through and lay
flopping along the pier, with her open hands
still held towards me. Now I know that was the day
I lost my mind. She's followed me the way
a beggar could haunt a doorway. She's in my shade
whenever I feel empty or afraid.

Look at her now; by now she's growing old.
We hear her every night, that singing, through
the heartless air, carried on the cold
enchantment of the California dew,
futile and endless notes, a wordless clue
sent out over the deafened land. I wish,
sometimes, I'd thrown her back in like a fish,

when I saw her breasts. A mother! I still can't say
if my fishing hook killed it, or if she
dropped it in the struggle, but of course it died that day.
And I know wherever it fell, there must be
a shrinking in the waves, the hissing sea,
a crust of sand still thickening on the edge
of its quiet bones.

DAUGHTER

Yes, cradle the fallen head—
Most of the blood is on the floor—
It spilled more after he was dead—

And then the feast turned into sand—
I knew that I could charm them all—
He fell under my mother's hand—

Mother, you said it would be for you—
He judges me, for eternity—
This is the last job—I will do—

As long as I can twirl and spin—
The blood will trickle on my skin—
as well as yours—my only kin.

My only anchor? We both know.
You watched the dance, smiled "Salome"—
It was your wish—now we both know—

How is my mother's breast my doom?
I'll only finish my dance—when—
Your eyes are bloody—like this room—

STRANGERS

She turned to gold and fell in love.
She danced life upside down.

She opened her wild eyes again
and asked some strangers in.

The strangers felt her in and out.
They found her outsides thin.

Since her heart was still and hard,
they knocked her insides in.

WESTMINSTER

Among these aisles and these attentive pews,
as sunset lowers silk down through the shafts
of remembering light, your whispering voice calls

from the stone bed, where long-resounding rose
embroiders the marble bodies as you plead,
"It's not my face; take this pocked stone away."

The other soldiers still hold the stiff lances
of their endless sight-lines to the roof. But I
have seen your crumbling life. You need to die.

I read the ruthless carvings on the low
Scherezades of monuments—designed
to run the reader through with Latin words—

looming always, waiting, drawing drying tears
to halo lead and stone. Dust writes the huge
cold pages pushing, with silent black and gold,

toward your tumble of marble sheets. One-armed, you lie
beside your husband, your thinning fingers spread
on your crumbled nipple, waiting for the stone

and time to cover them. The stone will kneel.
Here, silt-heart kings and sand-bodied dukes,
holding lead in the church, and dark in your hands,

the dead time is over. It makes no life here.
My night is abandoning the night where you lie,
where she and he walked up an aisle to He.

COATLIQUE

She listens for breathing
around her in the night.
Below the mountain,
families are sleeping.
When will she wake
to bring the morning?
When will she birth
sun and stars?
When will her mist
give birth to the moon?

The skulls are breathing,
as quiet in her necklace
as darkness will keep them.

STILL LIFE

A sunny afternoon; think of Vermeer.
Here is the apple, here the rounding side
of the blue pitcher. On the scrubbed wood just here,
she puts the pitcher down, so that the slide
of drops against its lip catches what light
there is for pitchers here this afternoon.
She does not really see the drops, or quite
attend the blue. A common thing. But soon
the tide will turn, and salty smells will rise
to circle in the street, and to her ears
will come the voices. Then doorways to her eyes,
then other days than this—afternoons, years.
She will stop to hold this moment near,
and drop the pitcher, and betray Vermeer.

THE CIRCLED SAND

Oaks have thickened. Blackberries
untighten. Warmed stones
encircle the dense and swerving sand.

Years, and weeks and hours
have turned, while water lily petals
hid the surface, then submerged,
or got tangled in our paddles.

Maple hands pushed their green light through you.
Pine and maple trees moved past,
the water opened out,
and mist appeared on the water.

IN CITIES, BE ALERT

You may hear that your heartbeat is uneven
and let new tension climb around your shoulders,
thinking you've found the trick for going mad.
But try to keep a grip on where you are.

Remember: all around you is pure city;
try to stay alert. On the wide streets,
so empty late at night, streaking in glass,
the color of an alley, or the fall

of a sideways flicker from a neon sign
may utterly and briefly disconcert you—
but as you go, you'll find that noise is worse.
Prepare for noise. But never scream. Even tensing

ears too far in advance can sharpen sirens,
and as for horns. . . . When you're back to
your normal rhythm after such encounters,

just try to stay alert. You'll never know
exactly who is coming up behind you,
but the sudden movement of pedestrians
will finally, of course, be what disarms you.

INSECT

That hour-glass-backed,
orchard-legged,
heavy-headed will,

paper-folded,
wedge-contorted,
savage—dense to kill—

pulls back on backward-moving,
arching
high legs still,

lowered through a deep, knees-reaching,
feathered down
green will,

antenna-honest,
thread-descending,
carpeted as if with skill,

a focus-changing,
sober-reaching,

tracing, killing will.

THREE GENERATIONS OF SECRETS

Is the sound of my loud carrying life a knell
far across your small ocean? Do you share
the secret that the months keep hidden there?
Is my past-filled pregnancy a hungry shell?
I think I will turn metal, like a bell,
so you can clapper my voice out, to where
the silent memories will echo care
and speak again. We'll sound our double spell,
swinging; we'll swing back then, to forgive
my mother's curve around the angry past—
and then her mother's. They were smothered, bound
and quiet. But we'll speak, and you will live,
tolling and striking what we know at last,
until you ring aloud with newer sounds.

BRIGID

Ring, ring, ring, ring! Hammers fall.
Your gold will all be beaten
over sudden flaming fire
moving from you, the pyre. Sweeten
your cauldron, until the sun
runs with one flame through the day
and the healing water will sing,
linger on tongues, burn away.

SAPPHICS FOR PATIENCE

Look there—something rests on your hand and even
lingers, though the wind all around is asking
it to leave you. Passing the open passage,
you have been chosen.

Seed. Like dust or thistle it sits so lightly
that your hand while holding the trust of silk gets
gentle. Seed like hope has come, making stillness.
Wish, in the quiet.

If I stood there—stopped by an open passage—
staring at my hand—which is always open—
hopeful, maybe, not to compel you, I'd wish
only for patience.

INSIDE THE VIOLET

Beside the long hedge on my parents' drive,
where the gravel waited daily for their tires
to crunch it open, in the narrow band
of earth along the hedge that kept the loam's
thick secret from the shifting sun, I knew
a purple violet. It always grew there,
hanging its knotty shoulders in the shade
of large, more splendid leaves, its crumpled head
releasing toward the earth.

                  One day I crouched
to find its eye much closer than before
and stared inside. My own eye was lost
in the echoing hold of the raw deep I saw,
though my hands held back inside the driveway world
that slowed its pulse around me as loud sun
shattered all the gravel into shade
and tamped the earth. The middle of the violet loomed;
its heart was moving over me to hold
me like a violet, too. As its yellow, strong
throat turned to me and opened one more door,
defining light poured from a silent sun,
threading my face and choking my mouth, until
I stopped looking in violets.

PEARL

Reaching with eyes, they covered her as a girl,
leaving a grain of gaze, the irritant stare
women must cover everywhere, with pearl.

Even in her own room alone, she curled
back from the windows gleaming with their glare.
Reaching with eyes, they covered her, as a girl,

stopping her gaze with a long look, unfurled,
taking her in as if she belonged there,
a woman covered everywhere, with pearls

draping her throat, before she learned to whirl
beside the mirror, pierce her ears, or twine her hair.
Reaching with eyes, they covered her, as a girl

covers and hunches herself in, to coil
less of her toward the voyeur. But beware.
Women can cover everything, like pearls

orbed and alive. A living ocean swirls;
we encompass it and spiral everywhere.
Reaching with eyes, they covered, in the girl,
what the woman covers: everything, like pearl.

RAIN BIRTH

This is the rainy season, like a birth
around our windows. In your open eyes,
and in the heart whose hands, beating inside
my hands, have opened out, we meet the rain.
The quiet sentinels—the trees—unfold
outside the window. Light and cold
go running through the day. In the full tide
that loosens skies to water, in the sea
that comes to find me, I see your eyes,
and, perishing from salt, I dry my eyes.

NUT

I cry for my lost days, I cry for my childhood,
I cry for the goddess coming down from the sky.
I cry for a place on the ground for my feet
and I call for a place on the ground for my hands.
In the daylight my hands reach out for home;
in the night, the stars connect the stones
and find their way. The shooting stars
fall from your breasts, your arms.

FROZEN IN

Venice, December

Ours are the only mouths
to taste with this smothering slow
touch, and the only steps
to sink like bellsounds and cave
deep into the marble snow.

Women who go to the window
to push their arms out to the snow
and then bring the shutters back in
follow us as we fall
past their eyes where the black night lives.

We are snowflakes at last, where the thick
never locked, never closed doors
follow us through squares of light
that windows have left on the snow.
Once again, warmth that falls,
again, though our tracks fill and slow.

THE GARDEN

Out of old earth where the worms have eaten,
the grim garden begins to grow.
When peas, dull dragons, unwind and dip
rough leaves the land has licked,

lulled by a dust of lingering crumbs
dropped by the tongue of the turned-up
underground, hunched over the earth,
beans bend and bow, like figureheads.

Raise them roaring, ribbon sun,
beat them open, oar them out
far to sea. They'll face furrows
through the wind. They'll walk waves.

ANOTHER RELUCTANCE

Chestnuts fell in the charred season,
fell finally, finding room
in air to open their old cases
so they gleam out from the gold leaves
in dust now, where they dropped down.

I watch them, waiting for winter,
husks open and holding on.
Their rusted rims are rigid-hard
but cling soft to the clear brown.
This low light sinks soon

from the old tree in the only sun,
from the gifts that have fallen. Cold children's
chestnuts, hidden in small caches,
have gone hollow, with gleams gone,
grain gone, now the children are home.

TRIBUTE

"You'll find—it when you try to die—"
—*Emily Dickinson*

When there are no words left to live,
I have elected hers

to haunt me till my margins give
around me, web and bone.

Her voice has vanished through my own.
She makes me like a stone

the falling leaves will sink and stay
not over, but upon.

APHRODITE

Aphrodite, come to me,
even while I lie resting with my infant.
Cover me with your sweet certainty.

COURTSHIP

Courtship is pulling with your full-moon heart
to bring out patterns. Patterns dry, crisp tides
that crescent up the beach, past sifted sand,
as sunset comes. When all the shores are dark,

night pulls with courtship's tides (Love leaves the tides
aside, to push on further up the sand,
to change far pools, to ebb into the heart
of earth and leave it salty, full, and dark).

COY MISTRESS

Sir, I am not a bird of prey:
a Lady does not seize the day.
I trust that brief Time will unfold
our youth, before he makes us old.
How could we two write lines of rhyme
were we not fond of numbered Time
and grateful to the vast and sweet
trials his days will make us meet?
The Grave's not just the body's curse;
no skeleton can pen a verse!
So while this numbered World we see,
let's sweeten Time with poetry,
and Time, in turn, may sweeten Love
and give us time our love to prove.
You've praised my eyes, forehead, breast:
you've all our lives to praise the rest.

BEING A CONSTELLATION

Heavy with my milk, you move
your compact body, though I hold
you dense under a constellation
whose sparse lights ache over you.

If, looking up, you recognize
the shadowing of curves that casts
toward my belly, and the way
my nipples travel, like two stars

twinned by your eyesight; if my arms
take night, and keep it from the sky,
if my night voice can stop your cry,
I'll be the Mother over you.

You are a question, small and dense,
and I am an answer, long diffuse
and dark, but I want to be sky
for you so, like the stars, I lie,

holding my far lights wide and flat
in pictures for your eyes to take,
spaced easily, so you can catch
the patterns in your sleepy net.

WALK WITH ME

Walk with me just a while, body of sunlight,
body of grass, surface of trees,
head bending to the earth we have tasted,
body of death, surface of leaves.
Sinking hooves in the mud by the river,
root of the live earth, live through my body.
Sinking body, walk in me now.

CHANGING WOMAN

If we change as she is changing,
if she changes as we change

(If she changes, I am changing)

Who is changing, as I bend
down to what the sky has sent us?

(Is she changing, or the same?)

ANCESTOR

Grizzel McNaught (1709–1792)

Bound in a chain of women, I
sometimes reach out with alarm,
and catch, sometimes, an old reply.

My chain connects me to the farm
that formed her ground, that fed her sheep.
The chain is just a Scottish charm,

but she grows frantic if I sleep.
The roots that dig around her tomb
deepen, till I reach to keep

the feel of her low-ceilinged room,
the branches that burst from her broom.

GULF WAR AND CHILD: A CURSE

You are sleeping, your fingers all curled,
your belly pooled open, your legs gathered, still
in their bent blossom victory.

I couldn't speak of "war" (though we all do),
if I were still the woman who gave birth
to you soft-footed, with your empty hand
and calling heart, a border of new clues.

May the hard birth our two heartbeats unfurled
for two nights that lasted as long as this war
make all sands rage, until the mouth of war
drops its cup, this bleeding gift we poured.

THANKSGIVING

for Julian

Earth is getting ready to harden and dim
in an unmoving winter. A dry yellow curl
bends the grasses the long year has tufted and brimmed.

Their tops start to flatten, hushed by the hurl
the wind sends through the trees, and soon they will bow.
Layered on grain, quick-shadowed like pearl,

sky-thick gray clouds anchor down to plow
the black plunging earth. As the furrows grow strange
and dark with their shadows, the morning grows. How

can a harvest this cold wrinkle open and change?
Laced into earth by their last anxious stalks,
the fields wait. Nothing's there, in the sky's empty range,

but the emptying wind that listens and talks,
or else barely stutters, stumbling by
on its way to bring snow. The day-darkened hawks

slow their long wheeling, up the thin sky,
and then push back downward with shuddering grace
to catch the dry answer this time makes. The high

piled grain, the bleached houses and barns, lean. You place
fourteen dense kernels of looming seed-corn
with care in my left hand. Their saffron-hard trace

of the sun is alive, a long memory torn
from a stalk. So smooth, they call quiet, as loud
as your opened eyes spoke the first day you were born.

THE WISH FOR EYES

On solid hills through liquid dusk,
the city turns to rise

with its purple touch, to enter me.
I touch it with my eyes.

Gray nature, make a dusk of me,
and let me keep my ties.

Though I am solid, even hard,
touch me back with my eyes.

EVE

When mother Eve took the first apple down
from the tree that grew where nature's heart had been
and came tumbling, circling, rosy, into sin,
which goddesses were lost, and which were found?
What spirals moved in pity and unwound
across our mother's body with the spin
of planets lost for us and all her kin?
What serpents curved their mouths into a frown,
but left their bodies twined in us like threads
that lead us back to her? Her presence warms,
and if I follow closely through the maze,
it is to where her remembered reaching spreads
in branching gifts, it is to her reaching arms
that I look, as if for something near to praise.

ENCOUNTER

Then, in the bus where strange eyes are believed to burn
down into separate depths, ours mingled, lured
out of the crowd like wings—and as fast, as blurred.
We brushed past the others and rose. We had flight to learn,
single as wings, till we saw we could merge with a turn,
arching our gazing together. We formed one bird,
focused, attentive. Flying in silence, we heard
the air past our feathers, the wind through our feet, and the
    churn
of wheels in the dark. Now we have settled. We move
calmly, two balanced creatures. Opened child,
woman or man, companion with whom I've flown
through this remembering, lost, incarnate love,
turning away, we will land, growing more wild
with solitude, more alone, than we could have known.

SAMHAIN

In the season leaves should love,
since it gives them leave to move
through the wind, towards the ground
they were watching while they hung,
legend says there is a seam
stitching darkness like a name.

Now when dying grasses veil
earth from the sky in one last pale
wave, as autumn dies to bring
winter back, and then the spring,
we who die ourselves can peel
back another kind of veil

that hangs among us like thick smoke.
Tonight at last I feel it shake.
I feel the nights stretching away
thousands long behind the days,
till they reach the darkness where
all of me is ancestor.

I turn my hand and feel a touch
move with me, and when I brush
my young mind across another,
I have met my mother's mother.
Sure as footsteps in my waiting
self, I find her, and she brings

arms having answers for me,
intimate, a waiting bounty.
"Carry me." She leaves this trail
through a shudder of the veil,
and leaves, like amber where she stays,
a gift for her perpetual gaze.

DIVING PAST VIOLETS

These words and I don't see you, though we charge
like horses past your tumid living stems,
stepping behind our braided forelocks, down
the paths your stems make, rooting underground.

Our tails move last into the mossy dirt,
swishing the last ray of daylight off.
How else could we approach? I knew I'd end
with winding, deep inside such patient caves.

NOTES

"*Rhiannon*" Rhiannon was a Welsh goddess often depicted as a girl riding a white horse. Associated with an older Celtic horse-goddess, she kept magic birds that sang the dead to life and the living to sleep.

"*No Snake*" Though the snake was originally sacred to the goddess in Western culture—as it still is worldwide—this poem responds to the snake story in Genesis. Books discussing how and why the symbolism of the snake changed include Merlin Stone's *When God was a Woman*, Mary Condren's *The Serpent and the Goddess*, and Maria Gimbutas's *Lady of the Beasts*.

"*Spider Woman*" An important being in many Native American cultures, Spider Woman was the thoughtful weaver who created the sun and fire and people, who remain connected to her through threads of spider silk. The chant form of this poem has Native American influences.

"*Inanna*" The subject of the most ancient extant written poems, Inanna was worshipped for 3500 years as the "Queen of Heaven and Earth" in ancient Sumer. The story of her journey to the underworld—for three days and nights—and her rebirth is recounted in many hymns, stories, and carvings, which are collected in Wolkstein and Kramer's *Inanna: Queen of Heaven and Earth* and discussed in Sylvia Brinton Perera's *Descent to the Goddess* and elsewhere. The four-beat accentual line, divided into two parts, was common in Sumerian poetry.

"*The Last Mermother*" Since the mermaid "descends from very old traditions connecting Goddess figures with the sea as universal womb," to quote Barbara Walker's *Woman's Dictionary of Symbols*, the idea of a mermother may not be as strange as I thought when it first came to me. Sources underlying this poem include Kim Chernin's *The Hungry Self*, Dorothy Dinnerstein's *The Mermaid and the Minotaur*, Alice Miller's *Drama of the Gifted Child*, and Elaine Morgan's *The Descent of Woman*.

"*Daughter*" Matthew 14:6-8 recounts how Salome, whose dancing had pleased Herod so much that he told her to ask for anything she wanted, was ordered by her mother to demand the head of John the Baptist on a silver platter. Salome is present with the three Marys at the death of Jesus as described in Mark 15:40.

"*Coatlique*" Coatlique is the oldest pre-Columbian deity, mother of the Aztec gods, the earth goddess who destroys living things so they can be reborn. Associated with the snake, she consumes the sun each night and births it each morning. Depictions of her are decorated with skulls.

"*Brigid*" Called the "bright one," Brigid was the divine ancestor of the Irish Celts, worshipped continually until the 18th century. Brigid had three aspects, as the goddess of healing, the goddess of smithcraft and metalwork, and the goddess of poetry and inspiration who taught people how to whistle and how to write. The form of this poem is a Welsh form, the Awdl Gywydd.

"*Nut*" An ancient African goddess of the cosmos who survived into Egyptian mythology, Nut arches over the world with her hands and feet on the earth, and the rain flows from her breasts. Each night she swallows the sun, which travels through her body all night until she gives birth to it again in the morning.

"*Aphrodite*" Though later identified with erotic love only, Aphrodite is associated with such powerful pre-Hellenic creator/destroyer goddesses as Astarte, Ishtar, and Isis.

"*Coy Mistress*" is an imaginary response to Andrew Marvell's famous seduction poem: "The grave's a fine and private place, / But none, I think, do there embrace .... An hundred years should go to praise/thine eyes, and on thy forehead gaze;/Two hundred to adore each breast, But thirty thousand to the rest. . . ."

"*Changing Woman*" Among the Apache, Changing Woman was the constantly self-transforming earth-goddess who always stayed young, by walking towards the east until she met and merged with her younger self.

"Eve" Though Eve may be seen as a symbol of the demonization of women, she shares many characteristics with the ancient mother-goddesses worldwide from whom her story derives. Like her predecessors, Eve brought both death and life to humanity. In some Judeo-Christian legends, she also persuaded God to allow humans to be resurrected.

"Samhain" Samhain is the Celtic Hallowe'en celebration, the start of the new year in the traditional pagan calendar, a time when interaction between the worlds of the living and the dead is believed to be easier than at other times.

Annie Finch is author of two poetry chapbooks, most recently *Catching the Mermother* (Aralia Press), and a book on poetics, *The Ghost of Meter: Culture and Prosody in American Free Verse* (Michigan). She has also edited the anthology *A Formal Feeling Comes: Poems in Form by Contemporary Women*. Her poems have appeared in *Paris Review, Kenyon Review, Agni Review, Southwest Review, Partisan Review, Puerto del Sol*, and elsewhere, and she is currently translating the works of French Renaissance poet Louise Labé. She earned her B.A. at Yale and doctorate at Stanford, and teaches on the creative writing faculty at Miami University in Ohio (finchar@muohio.edu/http://www.muohio.edu/~finchar/).